# Sit, dip, tip

Nat sits.

Dan sits.

Sam dips in.

Sam tips Nat and Dan in.

# Sit, dip, tip

Level 1, Set 2: Story 1

# Before reading

**Say the sounds:** s a t p i n m d
Ensure the children use pure sounds for the consonants without the added "uh" sounds, e.g. "mmmm" not "muh".

**Practise blending the sounds:** sit dip tip Nat sits Dan Sam dips tips
**High-frequency words:** am in  **Tricky words:** I and
**Vocabulary check:** dip – when you dip into a pool, you dive or jump in

**Story discussion:** What do you think the boys are doing on the cover?

**Teaching points:** Check that children can say the phonemes /s/ /a/ /t/ /p/ /i/ /n/ /m/ /d/, and that they can identify the grapheme that goes with each phoneme.
Check they understand that speech bubbles are sometimes used to hold the words that characters say in stories.
Point out the tricky words "I" and "and", and practise reading them together.

# After reading

**Comprehension:**
- Where does this story take place?
- What does Nat sit on?
- What happens when Sam gets into the pool?
- How do you think the children feel at the end of the story?

**Fluency:** Speed-read the words from the inside front cover.